BUDD

PRAYERS & MANTRAS

America Selby

Ladies Image Publishing

Email: americaselby@outlook.com

Dear Reader,

If you enjoyed this book or found it useful, I would be very grateful if you would post a short review on Amazon. Your support really does make a difference and I read all the reviews personally so I can get your feedback and make this book even better.

If you would like to leave a review, all you need to do is click the review link on this book's Amazon page here.

If you are a member of kindleunlimited, I would be most grateful if you would scroll to the back of the book so I will be paid for your borrowed book.

Thanks again for your support.

America Selby

How do Buddhists Pray?

Buddhist prayer is often more meditation, such as focusing on giving loving kindness to other people; therefore, Buddhists often pray by repeating certain mantras. Many Buddhists, such as those who practice Nichiren Buddhism, offer prayers to awaken the divinity inside themselves. Buddhists do not pray to a god or divine being outside of themselves because Buddhists generally believe that divinity is inside each person. For example, Nichiren Buddhists sometimes chant various texts, such as the mystic law's name or parts of the Lotus Sutra. This type of prayer is to encourage divine qualities in the person, such as courage or wisdom. Tibetans repeat mantras to open themselves up to a different type of consciousness, while some Japanese Buddhists offer prayers to Amida Buddha, who is the Buddha of Infinite Light. They pray to Amida Buddha in hopes that they will join the Amida Buddha in the Pure Land.

Buddhist Prayers

Buddhism is a religion of the mind. Much in the same way that water ripples fade, so too does Buddhism see the nature of the mind. In Buddhist philosophy, the four noble truths are the descriptions of reality revealed by the Buddha. Dissatisfaction. The cause of dissatisfaction. The end of dissatisfaction. And how to get there. The way to end dissatisfaction is called the Eightfold Noble Path and is the formula for generating only good things rather than bad, and avoiding dissatisfaction. This leads into the idea of the Triple Gem. The Triple Gem is the language used within Buddhism to describe three things. The Buddha. The Dharma. And the Sangha. The Buddha is the teacher, and also represents the potential all of us have for becoming free from our suffering. The Dharma is the teachings he revealed. And the Sangha is the community to which you can go to for support in following the path.

These prayers will honor various beings known as Bodhisattvas. In several traditions of Buddhist thought, Bodhisattvas are people who are almost at Enlightenment, or the end of dissatisfaction, but stay. They stay not out of doubt or fear but out of compassion for those who they would leave behind. They vow to stay within the cycle of suffering in order to liberate the beings around them first. The prayers will also honor the Triple Gem, and the nature of the mind. Within these prayers there will be mantras used to focus the mind and to condense the teachings of a particular idea into a simple phrase. The prayers will also be written in the style of traditional Buddhist prayers, and as such will use a lot of Buddhist terminology.

PRAYER ONE

Om Muni Muni Maha Muni Shakyamuni Svaha. Lord Buddha, guiding light and beacon through the terrors of Samsara, I honor you. Noble teacher, you spent years torturing your body for the sake of the mind's liberation. You spent your childhood surrounded by opulence. And when you awakened you saw the middle ground. Help me to walk the narrow edge of Dharma. I need you to hold my hand and guide me, for my mind is cloudy and I cannot see. All around me people are starving while some eat with endless waste. My heart hurts with compassion. Help me to extend that compassion to both the suffering of the starving and the ignorance of the greedy. May all beings be happy. Help me, Lord Buddha, to see as you do. Let the Buddha nature within me blossom and come forth, bursting through the world like a crack of lightning. Let all my actions be of good merit and bring forth good karma in my life. Let me escape my dark habits, the karma of lives lived. Let me become a Buddha for the benefit of all sentient beings. The starving cry with helplessness while the arrogant ones eat their fill and more. Let me be a Buddha, to show them that there is no you, or us, but the eternity of the stillness of the mind. Let me become a lamp to show them the way to freedom. Lord Buddha in your dying words you said, "be a lamp unto yourself, strive on with diligence." Help me to strive against the negative forces of our consequences, and free all beings from despair.

PRAYER TWO

I prostrate reverently before the Triple Gem. The world around me churns with suffering and still I bow before Buddha, Dharma, and Sangha. Terrorism tears the beings on this Earth apart. I bow to the Buddha. We see two sides, but really it is a mirror. I bow to the Dharma. We are disconnected and unable to seek peace. I bow to the Sangha. I bow to myself, for within I hold the seeds of the Triple Gem, drawing upon it in order to sow peace wherever I am. Fear rules the world, but I bow. I bow for suffering. I bow for terrorism. I bow towards all sides. I bow towards disconnect. I bow towards fear. Within this world I wait in hope for when my actions draw forth enough merit to break free from the chains that bind me to Samsara and shine with the eternal light of an awakened Buddha. That Buddha in the future is the me in the here and now. I just have yet to see it. My mind is filled with fears and thoughts the way a still pond is agitated by thrown stones. I see no peace. But still I bow. I bow for all sentient beings and proclaim the Dharma. Duality is a lie. There is no fight. We are fighting our own minds. All of us locked in struggle with the same enemy. This we do not know, and it rips us apart. We fight each other, letting the enemy win. The Triple Gem shines like a beacon, and I bow to it.

PRAYER THREE

Om Mani Padme Hum. Avalokitesvara, Chenrezig. Kuan Yin. Bodhisattva of Compassion, I beseech you. I bow before your splendor, compassionate one. I am lost in the whirlwind of Samsara. Hear my cries, and stretch out your thousand arms towards me. You are my refuge within the rushing tide. The three poisons pollute my mind and I cannot think. I cannot see. Everything is clouded. But I prostrate before you, wishing for your peace. Grant me the gift of bodhicitta so that I may too give up my Enlightenment for the noble cause of the Nirvana of all sentient beings. You are so honorable and powerful, you hold open the door to Enlightenment, postponing your own freedom from rebirth by allowing all others to pass through before you. The might of your awakened mind burns down into the hell realms and soars through the heavens. You are the shining hope of the hopeless, the compassionate heart of an Awakened One. My heart overflows with desire for the peace that comes within the realization of the compassionate mind of bodhicitta. I am restless in Samsara and despise my karmic debts. Avalokitesvara, I bow before you who represent freedom from the hate and aversion that binds so many people in our day. I throw myself to your mercy for Samsara flows around me in a bitter rush, and I see no end. Death is everywhere, and ignorance rips apart the mind. But you are there so I will cry out, and you will listen.

PRAYER SIX

All around me flows the ups and downs of Karmic consequences. I shiver and shake, adrenaline coursing through me as I face my fears. I stare into the void of myself and I scream, ripping apart my ego. I ask the ten thousand Buddhas to cover me with their compassionate hands, holding me up as I writhe in endless battle with the devils of the mind. I fight myself, the illusion that I hold most dear, and I fight the three poisons in deadly combat. With the sword of the awakened mind I go to battle. Dearest Buddhas, I ask that you stand with me as I endeavor towards freedom. May you always stand next to the striving, and reach out with endless offering hands to give those who search for Enlightenment aid. I am walking in the blind darkness of ignorance, but I wish to see with the clarity of a Buddha. I am stricken with trembling fear as my ego screams with terror as I take my hesitant steps into the way of the Dharma. To kill the ego is to realize Nirvana. In every way let my actions bear fruit to aid me in my endless endeavor. Help me as I strive towards Nirvana, and help me too, once I gain the awakened mind, to hold open the door for others. I proclaim unto you my heartfelt desire for Enlightenment. Help me to rid myself of the ego's illusionary fears, walking boldly towards the Supreme Enlightenment, hand in hand with those who make up the Sangha.

PRAYER SEVEN

In reverence I bow respectfully to all the venerable monks, nuns, and teachers within the Sangha. I thank you for your precious example on rightful living and generating good merit. I thank you for the opportunity to hear you expound upon the venerable teachings in which the Buddhadharma is laid clear for me because of your merits. I follow your example in my life, as a placeholder when I am led astray. I am filled with outside distractions in an age where quiet peacefulness is lost amidst the raucous screaming of the intellectual and technological age. Within your model I can rest in ease amidst the teachings of the Buddha, free from distractions, focused wholly on following you in what I must do to free myself from worldly errors. You are a generator for good karma, allowing me to fall into the appropriate patterns that dictate a peaceful human rebirth within the Dharma. Your life of structured adherence to the precepts of the ordained life give me resolve to focus within myself for the strength to follow my own precepts, those which are of such small number and weak of demand in comparison with your own mighty task. By meditating upon you, may I become more like your model and your example, and gain the everlasting peace of Enlightenment. I thank you for being here for me, in every way, and for directing me in my path upon the Dharma's illustrious journey. May you live long, and lead many after you, towards the light of Nirvana.

PRAYER EIGHT

Lord Buddha, help me as I awaken today. Let every action be a mindful one, and every thought be one of loving-kindness. May like a courtly gesture, all of my actions be schooled and dictated with humble realization. Let my heart encompass all sentient beings as I walk through my daily life. As I stumble into situations: I can't find my keys, my significant other is being hard to talk to, a coworker is difficult, let me face all of these things and more, as I walk through my life with mindfulness. When I can't find my keys, let me center of my breath, giving me clarity to find them with efficiency. When my significant other is being hard to talk to, let me crush my idea of separateness and meet them where they are. When a coworker is being difficult, let me let go of the idea that they should act in a certain way. All of the struggles I will face today are bred from my own mind. If someone cuts me off on my way to work, the struggle is present if I react negatively. But seeing with the clarity of mindfulness, I will let go of my perceptions, and fall gracefully into the knowledge of interconnectivity. My light shall be my mindfulness, but I cannot do it alone. Lord Buddha, you who are the One Who Has Gone Before, aid me in my daily tests and faults, show me the instructions of the shining Dharma where I cannot see it, and lead me with your glorious revelation of freedom, onwards and upwards, throughout my life.

PRAYER NINE

Oh how horrid the depths of Samsara! I cry out for liberation! Liberation! The wretched cycle of rebirth and death disgusts me! No longer shall I watch those I care for pass away! No longer shall I weep and groan under the karmic load I carry! I cast it away from me! In the presence of all the Buddhas and Bodhisattvas, I proclaim my intent for freedom. I shall no longer be a slave of this meaningless, endless cycle. I turn to the Dharma with fierce determination. I shall be liberated. With righteousness I task myself with the precepts, following the noble eightfold path towards my lofty goal. I generate karma for good, and to fling myself higher and higher at Nirvana. My next life I refuse to waste. I shall generate karma that will make life easier for the next person I become. There is no end and no beginning, only the endless war I cry out at Samsara. No more shall I bear weighty burdens under the whip of the task masters of Ignorance, Attachment, and Hatred. I am free of them! I throw them off, and smash them to the ground as offerings of liberation to the Buddhas and Bodhisattvas. The Buddhas beckon and the Bodhisattvas light the way. The path is ahead of me and I stride forward boldly. With the Dharma in all I do I wage war against my own mind, and I swear I shall triumph. I shall join the ranks of the countless Buddhas and bring peace and compassion to all sentient beings. This is my oath. This is my war.

PRAYER TEN
(Great Compassion Mantra Prayer)

The world is full of division. Namo Ratna Trayaya Namo Arya. Police brutality divides citizens from those who swore to protect them. We are all hurrying about our separate ways, increasingly disconnected from each other. Valokite Svaraya Bodhisattvaya. We are a people lost and mindless. Crying out for aid, we stretch our hands in all directions. Mahasattvaya. Our minds are filled with greed for more and more material things. Mahakarunikaya, Om, Sarva Raviye. There is no end to Samsara. It stretches out in front of us as we drag our tired bodies down the path, bearing our karmic loads above us. Sudhanadasya, Namas Krtva Imam Arya. As we step heavily down the path, our minds fixed with desperation on freedom, the Bodhisattva Guan Yin appears. Valokite Svara Ramdhava, Namo Narakindi. She opens her arms and gathers us into them. Oh beautiful Lady of the Dharma! Offerer of dew drops on the foreheads of the oppressed! Hrih Mahavat Svame, Sarva Arthato Subham. Thank you for showing us the way to Enlightenment. You take our karmic loads, face smiling. Ajeyam, Sarva Sat Namo Vasat Namo Vaka. All the deeds we've done in the past, you lift them from our shoulders and take them upon yourself, walking upright and as lovely as a young deer. Mavitato, Tadyatha, Om Avaloki, Lokate, Krate, E Hrih. I too aspire to be like Guan Yin, protector of those imprisoned in Samsara.

PRAYER ELEVEN

(Part Two of the Great Compassion Mantra Prayer)

Mahabodhisattva, Sarva Sarva, Mala Mala, Mahima Hrdayam. We meditate dutifully as the Buddha said, minds concentrated in holy rage against Samsara. Kuru Kuru Karmam. Guan Yin, I call you to my aid, please, help me in my struggle against separation. Dhuru Dhuru Vijayate. I don't want to be alone in this world, and my Samsara trapped mind cannot see my indivision. Maha Vijayate, Dhara Dhara, Dhrni. Help me, Oh Compassionate One, I need to be free from the illusions that rule my life! Svaraya, Cala Cala, Mama Vimala. I shrug off my karmic load, letting it fly away in the boundless light of the Bodhisattva's compassionate glance. Muktele, Ehi Ehi, Sina Sina, Arsam Prasali. I swiftly cut my ties with my attachments. Visa Visam, Prasaya, Hulu Hulu Mara. Destroying temptation, I am floating in boundless mindfulness. Hulu Hulu Hrih, Sara Sara, Siri Siri, Suru Suru. Guan Yin, your beautiful face awakens a longing in me for the sweetness of Enlightenment. Bodhiya Bodhiya, Bodhaya Bodhaya, Maitreya, Narakindi, Dhrsnina, Vayamana. I take refuge from my karma in the arms of all the Buddhas, seeking peace from my suffering.

PRAYER TWELVE
(Part Three of the Great Compassion Mantra Prayer)

Svaha, Siddhaya, Svaha, Mahasiddhaya, Svaha. I develop the good karma to be able to break free from dependent origination. I am no longer tied to my mistakes, fettered to my suffering by chains of habitual mistakes. Siddhayoge, Svaraya, Svaha. Sights set upon the thousands of Buddhas on their gold thrones, surrounded by perfume, I bow in reverence. Narakindi, Svaha, Maranara, Svaha. All around me, Enlightened beings rest in perfect harmony. Sira Simha Mukhaya, Svaha. I am one of them. As the words of this mantra flow through me, let the Buddha-nature within my being blossom into brilliant reality. Sarva Maha Asiddhaya, Svaha. Guan Yin inclines her head to me, offering a step up onto an empty throne. Cakra Asiddhaya, Svaha. In freedom I recline, sending out rays of light towards all beings who live in ignorance. Padma Kasiddhaya, Svaha, Narakindi Vagalaya. I raise a hand and a cool wind blows, smothering the fires of hatred. Svaha, Mavari Sankharaya. With a sharp motion, I cut off the ties of attachment of all suffering beings. Svaha, Namo Ratna Trayaya. Sickness and death are no more. The words of Guan Yin's Enlightened mantra burn away all illness among sentient beings. Namo Arya, Valokite, Svaraya, Svaha. The countless Buddhas offering their hands to the multitudes stuck in Samsara. Om Sidhyantu, Mantra, Padaya, Svaha. Countless Bodhisattvas bow at the words of the mantra. I gaze with serene countenance at all of existence. I am awake.

PRAYER THIRTEEN

Lord Buddha, I cannot think. I cannot feel. I feel as if a weight is upon my chest and I cannot remove it. Dread fills me and all I can see are the thousands of errors I've done in all my lives. I feel fear like no other, and Samsara closes in around me with the prospect of having to do this trial called life all over again. Lord Buddha, help me! I go to the Dharma and its words offer what I seek, but my mind is so clouded by karma that I cannot practice. I go to the Sangha, but I stumble, unable to connect with fellow practitioners. My meditation practice dwindles, and I fall deeper into attachment. Lord Buddha, help me to rip my mind from the vise my karma has set it in. Give me the strength to stand up and walk towards the Dharma, shaking off my ignorance as I set out on the path towards Enlightenment once more. As I do so, let me see that my hands have never been disconnected from those of the Sangha, I've been supported all along. Lord Buddha, you sat with ferocious diligence until your Enlightenment. In this manner, let me attack my own karma, and ruin the effects of the Three Poisons forever. I walk in the darkness of ignorance, unable to break free. Lord Buddha, give me the courage I need to rip myself away from my many attachments, seeking the freedom of the Dharma in all things.

PRAYER FOURTEEN

As cool water sits in a still pool, so too is my mind. I am a pristine mirror, thoughts floating like clouds in the sky above me! At ease I rest in my own being, allowing and not resisting. I am peacefulness, the quiet moments in-between thoughts. All around me the world rages, Samsara's insistent shouting. But in perfect faith. In perfect trust, I place my mind upon nothing else! I am nothingness. I am liberation! In peaceful happiness I sit, mind a blank slate! Nothing shall disturb this calm, nothing shall break or bend it. For I am this calm, and through it all, it is me and nothing else. Nothing can end it because it never began, it has always been there, I've just been ignorant of it. I turn to the Dharma, mind like a still pool, I practice with measured devotion! In every way I control my mind, and in this manner I live. Like a Buddha I walk the street with ease, mindful of every step. I turn to the people around me with joy, like a Bodhisattva I give them aid! But then a difficult person enters, the still pool is filled with waves. I see my world around me shattering, as karmic debts do be paid... But I am still that still pool. I am still peace. I accept the waves, watching them fade and fall back into being. I am the cool water in a still pool, my mind is as such always! The waves are only here for a short while, only to be gone the next day. I am free of all qualifications, quantifications, and creations! I am nothingness. I am liberation!

PRAYER FIFTEEN

Daring to walk amidst the suffering of Samsara, the compassionate Bodhisattvas tend to the pains of all sentient beings. Among our hatred, ignorance, and attachment, they stand gleaming. Thank you, oh mighty Bodhisattvas, for staying with us. I turn my mind to your perfection amidst my attachment and I feel your presence moving me to freedom. I turn my eyes with happiness upon your glorious vision, burning away my hatred. You walk among us, sincere and holy, Enlightened but intent on nothing else other than our Enlightenment before you too attain Nirvana. Above all else, you are the glorious rescuers of the struggling, suffering, and disillusioned. In my sorrow, you are there. In my joy, you are there. Oh great Bodhisattvas, your many arms are reaching towards me in perfect love. I wish that I were to join you, to aid all beings. But I myself need saving and so I kneel before you, clinging to my suffering as you, in great compassion, pry it relentlessly from my fingertips. I scream and I wail in my attachment, ignorant of the compassion you extend to me in my moment of pain. You rip my suffering from me, and I see myself clearly. You are the reason for my liberation, you great ones that wait for us, holding wide the way to Nirvana. I thank you, in all that I do, for your eternal sacrifice, until all sentient beings have attained Enlightenment. You are the bringers of peace, and I kneel in humble thanks.

PRAYER SIXTEEN

Lord Buddha, there is so much suffering in the world. People's greed overcomes them and becomes a beast that devours all the good in their lives. Karma etches itself into our every step, and our minds cannot see an end to the mindless cycle we take up every day of our wretched lives. The joys and happiness we gain briefly illuminate our minds, and give us a taste of the freedom you offer, but even those moments end. Our attachments drag us further into the murk, and Mara waits on every turn. When the joys end we race after them with desperate longing, our attachment to the brilliance of those moments sinking us deeper into Samsara's dreadful muck. How can we let go of even our happiness? Lord Buddha, you gave us the way, but we need to find a way to properly follow it. To let go of the whole and enjoy the single moment we will taste joy in all way do, losing our attachments to what then would become regular. I wish with heartfelt longing, to be free from my desire for happiness. I search, and search, and make mistakes, and all just ends in desperate fear. I wish to follow your noble path and live rightly, ridding myself of my attachments, and growing free of my ignorance.

PRAYER SEVENTEEN

Lord Buddha, be present as an ever present reminder of the power of the Dharma to those who live in ignorance. I ask this for those who fight their own family. I ask this for those who turn weapons against the innocent. I ask this for all who are victims in any way. This heartfelt prayer is for victims of domestic violence, of racism, of divide. May all sentient beings turn to the Dharma and find freedom within its noble teachings. As we turn towards pleasures and avoid pains, we create division and illusion around ourselves. Oh Tathagata, Buddha, you who have gone before us, spread the teachings of the Dharma to the hearts of these victims, and to my heart as well, for I am a victim of my own perception. Grant me peace from my struggles, and clarity to overcome my attachments. To the victims of the world, I pour out every good thing. In lovingkindness my heart opens up with bountiful charity. In everything I do I embody the Dharma, spreading it to those in need. And so with this honorable attitude, I become the hand of the Buddha to spread good things to all beings. In this honorable attitude my Buddha-nature grows and flourishes, and thus in doing good to others, I do good to myself. Tathagata Buddha, your warm smile sends all thoughts of attachments from my mind. You show me that peace and love are attainable, and that freedom from the endless cycle of suffering is the highest ideal. In this way, I help others and do homage to your exalted example.

PRAYER EIGHTEEN

My mind swirls and whirls around itself, laughing crazy; monkey mind. I try to sit on my meditation cushion and tame it but it springs out of reach, bubbling with endless thoughts. Did I wash the dishes? Did I do this? Did I pay that bill? The thoughts of life's ceaseless noise ripple through my brain, causing fury and frustration. But then, when one eye peels itself open despite my desperation, it falls upon the statue of Lord Buddha in front of me. His serene countenance. His calm posture. The promise of Enlightenment that his figure illuminates. And the monkey mind grinds to a halt in awed wonder, respect, and surprise. I breathe in and out, the present moment large and looming. The sweet sensation of concentration wraps around me like a cloak. I sigh into it and then with a sudden shock, the monkey mind starts leaping again. Lord Buddha, in your example I sit and try to fight. Sometimes I gain victory over my mind, but mostly, I lose the battles. Help me to strive on no matter what and to be able to see that the monkey mind doesn't need taming, for it is in the action of attempting to tame it that it gains all the more power. In your example, teach me to let go. Let go of meditation. Let go of wanting to subdue my mind. Just let go, and live wholly in the eternal now. Help me. Because when I do that, I'll be able to finally taste the hint of liberation that resting in meditative concentration gives. Help me, to let go. And with faith, I follow your example, aiming towards non-aiming.

PRAYER NINETEEN

Avalokitesvara, Compassionate One! I cry out to you and find you beside me already, as you always are. Great Bodhisattva, I feel the weight of Samsara on my shoulders. Children are killed, kidnapped, and stolen away even in our most secure societies. If the little ones of our race are not protected, even from their own kind, then what good is all our trappings of civilization? In your mercy, glorious Bodhisattva, give the world freedom from the distorted thinking that arises to induce such tragic events. It is my wish that these practices end and that the children who are victim of them are freed from the terrifying existence they are doomed to. Let the adults involved in these practices see their role in right view, and understand how their perversion has ruined the lives of the children they interacted with in their delusions. Let every little voice that cries out for help be heard, and let your compassionate heart stretch out towards all of them. Let the power of the Dharma cleanse the world of such evil, and let all of humanity join together in compassionate equanimity to put an end to these practices and the states of mind that lead to such practices forming. I cry out for you to help, not for my sake, but for the sake of those locked in such a tragic cycle. In this life they make the hell realms seem so close. It is hard not to only see the darkness in the world and to ignore where right action occurs. Open my mind to help in the ways I can, and open the hearts of the world to the plight of the stolen innocent.

PRAYER TWENTY

Bodily pains and bodily pleasures distract the mind and turn it away from the fierce concentration that battles back attachment. Sitting cross-legged on my meditation cushion, my back hurts. My knees hurt. My whole body is a playground for demons. I am on fire. My mind rushes like a frantic fireman, but is not eased. As my day progresses, pleasurable experiences cross my path and I follow them like a dog after a thrown stick. My heart burns with longing for freedom from the never ending tug of war that I have become trapped in. It drags me to a fro without sight of any reprieve. It is my darkness. But I stumble as it pulls me, falling to my knees in front of the Buddha. "Save me!" I cry. The Buddha just smiles and says "Be a lamp unto yourself." And then my mind, quivering with the knowledge that it alone can free me from my suffering, snaps into determined concentration. I am a warrior. Wisdom is my sword and compassion is my shield. With these things I fight back the armies of Mara. Pain and Pleasure are held at bay. I am from the line of Buddhas. I shall prevail. And in all things, the words of the Buddha resound within me. "Be a lamp unto yourself." These words are what shall guide me. They shall teach me, protect me, and empower me.

PRAYER TWENTY-ONE

We are a people divided. Racism puts blinders upon us. Oh noble Buddhas, I prostrate in honor of the freedom from distinctions you offer. There is an end of suffering. There is an end of hate. There is an end of ignorance. There is an end of attachment. In the freedom of Enlightenment there is no such thing as race. The mind sees no separation, there is no we, nor I, nor you, for such words are not necessary when there is not a distinction between them. Let all the sentient beings in Samsara, especially those in a human life, see that. Let all of humanity see that there is a way for racism to end. There is a way, and that way is compassion. In the light of unbiased, awakened compassion, nothing seems new, drastic, or bothersome. Everything merely is part of a greater mission. Behold, Buddhas, I offer my life as a symbol of the end of division. I vow to be present amidst Samsara as a being striving to live beyond division. Buddhas, your awakened minds see reality as it is and you offer this knowledge out of compassion for us who still wallow in rebirth. Beyond rebirth, beyond suffering, you are there, compassionately offering the Dharma, and guiding Bodhisattvas to our aid. How great you are, and how honorable! It is into this world that I am born. Into Samsara's grip. But you offer a wondrous chance, to be free! To be free of the division racism brings upon this world. Let this vision become reality, blossoming upon Samsara with the might of ten thousand suns. For all sentient beings I offer the merit accumulated by my vows and wishes here shared.

PRAYER TWENTY-TWO

Great Lady Tara, Queen of the Buddhas, I bow before you respectfully. In your different forms you teach humanity all they must know. Shining jewel of the Dharma, your gentle smile imparts a thousand years of wisdom. You who liberate those in darkness, I bow before you. Bodhisattva, shining like the sun, you are more lovely than the sunlight through rain. From your lips the Dharma drops like brilliant pearls, tumbling to the hands of sentient creatures. With tenderness you inspire within us the mind of a Buddha, and by your gentle touch you awaken our Buddha-nature. Well honored one, you are so lovely. My mind is drawn to your peacefulness. More so than your loveliness, the shining light of Dharma you hold within you dazzles me and puzzles the will. You are far beyond distinctions, Queen of the Buddhas, you offer succor to those in need. You who are known as the Mother of all Buddhas, you extend this motherly love to all sentient beings, guiding us to our Enlightened destiny. In my humble state I bow to you, ashamed of my karmic debts, but you free me from my shame, for my karmic debts are not my punishment- I have learned from them already. In my pain you are with me, and your arms guide my every action. My mind is clouded by ignorance and I see this not, oh Queen, but you open my eyes and I behold your honorable glory.

PRAYER TWENTY THREE

Fear rules this world. Ugly, beaten, and scarred. All sentient beings obey it, their minds tossed restless on a sea of unknown terrors. Their minds create monsters where none are, and all around them dangers lurk. But the reality is something much different. There is no disconnect. Sentient beings are all connected. Fighting against fear, they put up walls, not seeing how there is no beginning and no end of fear. No beginning and no end of separation. No beginning and no end of thoughts. Here in the Dharma's brilliant wisdom I peer at reality in shock. The world is wholly different from what I thought it to be. The world is unity. There is no separation between you or I. We or they. Fear causes this distinction. I honor my teachers who illuminate the Way for me, and for the Buddha who long ago battled Mara beneath the Bodhi tree. We are Enlightened beings. We just are Enlightened beings who have forgotten who they really are. Lord Buddha, you said so eloquently, "Oh nobly born, remember who you are!" We are sons and daughters of the Dharma. Kings and Queens of wisdom and honor. In the illusion of separation, we let these honors fall from our shoulders. But you awaken us, opening our eyes to the truth of reality. Freed from fear we strive on boldly. Free from fear we battle hate. Free from fear we see our unity. And beyond the walls of fear we shall live the Middle Way.

PRAYER TWENTY FOUR

Oh glorious Buddha, on the night of your Enlightenment you battled with the demon Mara, the lord of temptation. Mara rules Samsara with an iron fist, drawing sentient beings deeper and deeper into the hell realms. I am living within them, tormented by my karmic debts, writhing in suffering. My existence is pain, ruled by ignorance, attachment, and hatred. But then shining within the darkness you appear, your hand lifted in calming peace. You turn the wheel of the Dharma, preaching to us caught within the tormented realms of hells. Light enters our world. Ignorance falls away and we see where our attachments lead to hatred- thus suffering. We dutifully follow the Dharma, erasing our negative karma. Freeing ourselves from the wrongs of the past. As the Dharma swells within us, we are born higher and higher, soaring from the hell realms with each life, ever onwards to the realms of the gods. We attain godliness, practicing the Dharma, and our minds are awash in pleasurable circumstances. This is our greatest test yet. Our minds fall into attachment, and ignorance washes over us. We recreate our karma that leads to the hell realms, minds unknowing of the horrendous doom we set upon us. But then you reappear. The glorious teacher, expounding the Dharma with terrible purpose. Our minds are unclouded and we are freed once more. Soaring higher and higher, we pledge the Bodhisattva vow, remaining in Samsara for all sentient beings. Minds illuminated, we become what we wish to attain. And thus our karmic debts are permanently dissolved. But out of compassion we remain, fighting for Enlightenment for all beings.

PRAYER TWENTY FIVE

Om Muni Muni Maha Muni Shakyamuni Svaha. I bow to you, honorable Buddha, he who forded the river of Samsara and reached the other shore. You who returned to teach of the Dharma, offering Enlightenment to all beings. Oh gracious prince of the Shakya clan, out of compassion for the suffering of sentient beings, you displayed your wealth of knowledge and freed those who are bound by Samsara's chains. Broken free of cyclical existence, you ceased to repeat the sufferings of the world. But you returned and turned the wheel of Dharma, allowing all others to follow in your path. Glorious son of Enlightenment, you returned to offer wisdom to the masses, and thus Bodhisattvas arose to take their place by your side. They paused to turn back their benevolent gazes upon the sentient beings in Samsara, and forsaking their Enlightenment they return time and time again in compassionate determination to free us. Thank you for taking it upon yourself to fight Mara for your eternal Enlightenment, glancing upon us sentient beings, and returning to this realm to inspire others. You who are just a man like any other, who out of practicing the path you realized your own Enlightenment, gracious are you who returned to offer the path to all other sentient beings. In your glorious Enlightenment you shine as a beacon of possibility.

Please leave a review

Go to amazon.com and type in *America Selby* to find my books.

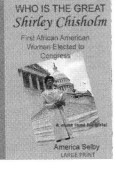

33155070R00018

Printed in Great Britain
by Amazon